I0617520

Leaving Behind:
A Literary Analysis Into the Mass Exodus of
Caribbean People

A Mental Rose Series Book

Author:
Tricia Monk, B.A., M.A., MS.Ed

Tri-State Logistic Essentials

Library of Congress Catalog
Monk, Tricia
Leaving Behind:
A Literary Analysis Into the Mass Exodus of
Caribbean People
A Literary Analysis Essay
A Mental Rose Series Book /
Tricia Monk 1st Ed.

English Language- Text/Picture Book

ISBN: 979-8-9855563-5-3

Dedication Page

God, the Most High, El Shaddai, Jehovah Jireh, my Guiding Light. Thank you for the blessings you have bestowed upon me and those I love greatly.

To the beautiful people of Haiti– from generations past, and generations to come. To my family, we are the chain breakers: stay authentic.

To exploration, to compassion, to diversity. Sharing the gift of culture and experience to the masses. This book is dedicated to you. Thank you for your support.

As recently as April 2023, one will notice that migration to specific countries has increased compared to recent past years: "Haitian migrants wade through a river as they cross the Darien Gap, from Colombia into Panama, hoping to reach the U.S., Oct. 15, 2022. The United States, Panama and Colombia announced Tuesday, April 11, 2023, that they will launch a 60-day campaign aimed at halting illegal migration through the treacherous Darien Gap, where the flow of migrants has multiplied this year" (Martinez). Migrants consist of men, women, and children, of all ages. Oftentimes these are families that have decided to take the treacherous journey of migration, despite the violence, hunger, vulnerability, and at times, even death, to reach Europe and/or the United States.

Effective January 6, 2023, President Biden, conducts a press release from the White House that announces that the United States Administration:

> … will extend the successful Venezuela parole
> process and expand it to nationals of Nicaragua, Haiti,

and Cuba. Up to 30,000 individuals per month from these four countries, who have an eligible sponsor and pass vetting and background checks, can come to the United States for a period of two years and receive work authorization. Individuals who irregularly cross the Panama, Mexico, or U.S. border after the date of this announcement will be ineligible for the parole process and will be subject to expulsion to Mexico, which will accept returns of 30,000 individuals per month from these four countries who fail to use these new pathways. Tripling Refugee Resettlement from the Western Hemisphere. The Biden-Harris Administration intends to welcome up to 20,000 refugees from Latin American and Caribbean countries during Fiscal Years 2023 and 2024, putting the United States on pace to *more than triple* refugee admissions from the Western Hemisphere this Fiscal Year alone. This delivers on the President's commitment under the *Los Angeles Declaration for*

Migration and Protection to scale up refugee admissions from the Western Hemisphere.

It appears that the United States' White House identifies the increased and persistent illegal migration concern, to foreign countries. Depending on the current situation, in a particular country, there can be several reasons why this risk is taken. Many supporters believe that this announcement is momentous as people from the approved countries will have the opportunity to make money, get an education, be with loved ones, have safety– in addition to other opportunities. Opposers question what will be left of the native country?-- A country of mass exodus. Only time will tell the impact of legalizing, and expediting the migration process for several countries– some perceived as "economically challenged" nations. Prior to examining the long-term impacts of "migration exodus",which this text will not cover, it is essential to evaluate the reasons/causes of why people of the Caribbean emigrate in such large numbers, as they often do.

Let's take a look at migration from the perspectives of literature written on the caribbean experience:

Background

The issue of Caribbean migration is evolving, as migration is increasing with time. Many theorists have tried to determine the factors that are contributing to the increasing numbers of Caribbean immigrants to the "States" and colonizing European nations; governed by the same government they've driven out and attained independence from in the past. Despite the Caribbean's attainment of national independence from Europeans, it appears through written and oral discourse, that the Caribbean islands and its people haven't fully acquired independence from the inferior conditions of their past; from which they are still suffering economically and socially. "The diaspora...has made Caribbean people an international people. In New York, Boston, Toronto, Montreal, London, Amsterdam, and Paris, communities have become established of people who regard their home as a distant island they may never see again, or barely remember, or remember in a way that has not existed for decades, "…Although the migratory experience has been painful for many Caribbean people, it has become a steadfast fixture of the Caribbean experience and a fixed element in the Caribbean economic system" (Kurlansky 220). This short analysis and photo-book will analyze the literature of Caribbean- migrant- authors, while exploring their theories underlying the inferior economic conditions, lifestyle differences, and the consistent migration of the Caribbean Islands.

Table of Contents

'Out of many one people' is Jamaica's national motto and it applies just as well to the rest of the Caribbean. The region's population is a rich mixture of African, European, American, Asian, and East Indian influences, its legacy a fusion of slavery, colonialism, and migration. This has created a unique culture, developed from centuries of interaction (Hamlyn 12).

Section 1: Introduction- Caribbean Literature

In an attempt to relay the Caribbean experience through its literature, Caribbean author Myriam J.A Chaney has established the various literary periods of, "Pioneers (born after WWI but publishing after WWII)…Nationalist (born before the mid 1930s, publishing during the independence period in the Caribbean)…Independence generation (born from the 1930s through 1940's and writing from the 1960s on)…and the Postcolonial (born from 1950 onward and publishing from the 1970's on)…" (Chaney 339). As a result of the histories that Caribbean people have undergone, much of their literature deals with the "Caribbean realities too often left unspoken: the voices of the poor, the female, and the neglected. Although most of the stories…speak of these issues and many of the authors are themselves of immigrant or poor backgrounds…, collection of those voices is undoubtedly canonical in its choices and historical organization. It does not lend room to the voices of spoken word poets, women's voices, or those who are of Caribbean descent but not born in the islands" (Chaney 340). Caribbean authors are in the best position to passionately and knowledgeably relay the Caribbean experience, including migration, views and concerns of everyday life, because that too is their reality:

> Writers have been among the professionals who have left. There has been an impressive outpouring of serious Caribbean literature in the second half of the twentieth century. Almost all of it is focused on the Caribbean, but frequently written from aboard. Exile, alienation, guilt, growing estrangement from home –these are persistent themes in modern Caribbean

literature. Poet Derek Walcott, whose plays and poems set daily Caribbean life into classical writing forms, has been living in Brookline, Massachusetts, and teaching poetry at Boston University. V.S. Naipaul of Trinidad, like Wilson Harris, has made his life in England. Jamaica Kincaid of Antigua settled in Vermont (Kurlansky 223)

Overall, Caribbean literature reflects the relevant situation of migration and the inadequateness of Caribbean life. Authors of Caribbean literature are plagued with the consistent notion of migration, whether it is personal or a mere reflection of Caribbean culture. Despite the fact that Caribbean literature, like other literary genres that focus on various subjects and concepts of the nature of the human condition, specifically consist of the people's want for a "better life" and their eventual migration to a land of a formal colonial power. Though this concept may not always be the main focus of a Caribbean piece, it always surfaces to some degree in the work.

In addition to the factor of migration, Caribbean islands' history, and people are all a conglomeration of exploration, exploitation, slavery, domination, and independence; therefore, it is inevitable that Caribbean literature/authors reflect these engrained factors in their work(s). Migration, on the other hand, is discussed in terms of the causes for-, circling back to the instabilities and problems of the nation itself.

The works and authors that will be the focus of this thesis represent only a few of the many Caribbean islands, and a small part of the complex concepts of migration. The authors explore the relevance of migration in the Caribbean, as well as the various reasons as to why many people of the Caribbean are willing to uproot themselves from their families, and lifestyle of many years. Caribbean writers explore the constant strive for survival because of the devastation of the Caribbean, and the tremulous life of the natives. In addition to relaying the concept of migration presented by the various authors, it explores the relevance of their theories as it relates to the historical context of the Caribbean.

Section 2: The Literary Common Thread of Migration

What is migration and what is its significance in the lives of Caribbean people? This is an inquiry that many Caribbeans ask themselves. Large numbers of legal and illegal Caribbean immigrants are reported to travel to the "States," and other colonizing countries in dangerous conditions, in large masses, and consistently, for various reasons. Many of these immigrants leave behind children, elderly parents, spouses, siblings etc., in hopes of establishing a life that would be of great benefit to themselves and those loved ones back in their native country. Caribbean authors, especially Austin Clarke, Edwidge Danticat, Earl Lovelace, and Makeda Silvera explore this great need and the normality of migration in their literary pieces.

Jamaican native Silvera, uses his rhyme-filled short-story, "Caribbean Chameleon" to illustrate the desire of migration amongst Caribbean people as indiscriminate throughout the various races, social classes, and religions. "Yard, Xamaica, Jamdown, Jah Mek Ya. JA. Airport. Gunman, mule, don, cowboy, domestic, refugee, tourist, migrant, farm worker, musician, political exile, business exile, economic exile, cultural exile, dreadlocks, locks-woman, fashion-dread, press-head, extension hair, haggler./ Leaving this Caribbean for the North Star...Destination America. Destination Britain. Destination Europe. Destination Canada. Destination foreign land... Immigration. Line long. Which one to enter. Woman or man. White or Asian. Black or White" (Silvera 399- 401). Silvera speaks of Caribbean people as one entity strongly dependent on migration to European countries.

Author Edwidge Danticat, in <u>The Dew Breaker,</u>
focuses on the various lives of Haitians who, despite their
many differences in religion, occupation, and social status,
share the same similarity of wanting to migrate to America.
Danticat uses the father, "the dew breaker," as the main focus
of her work. The "dew breaker," represents the many people
of Haiti who despite having taken full advantage of the land,
still long to leave the island. The "dew breaker," is a man
amongst the many "Volunteers of National Security." In the
text, he is referred to as "'Sergeant,' 'Colonel,' 'General.'
Some even blasphemously ennobled him 'Little President.'"
(Danticat 196). Considering this great honor or power, the
"dew breaker" still finds displeasure in his life and longs to
migrate.

> "…restaurants fed him an enormous amount of food,
> which he ate eagerly several times a day…A doctor,
> his landlord, gave him two rooms on the lower floor
> of a two-story house for free. Bourgeois married
> women slept with him…Virgins of all castes came

and went as well. And the people who had looked down on him and his family in the past…now…ask him for favors" (Danticat 196).

Danticat uses "the dew breaker's" exceptional societal status in society to show that even the ones that live desirable lives aren't sufficient enough to want to remain in the Caribbean. "He had been constantly thinking about getting out of this life, moving to Florida, or even New York, making himself part of the new Haitian communities there, to keep an eye on the movements that were fueling the expatriate invasions at the borders…He was already saving up his money to begin a new life…" (Danticat 189). Leaving one's familiar birth place for a foreign European land is much more desirable to Caribbean people. He represents the wealthy people, who also have the great aspiration to migrate from their island.

In contrast to the "Dew Breaker's," societal status within the Haitian population, are those inhabitants of the Caribbean living average lives, likely in severe poverty.

Danticat, skillfully, analyzes the lives of those citizens in relation to the common thread of Caribbean migration. Anne, another main character of the text, aspires migration, as an escape from the Caribbean life of uncertainty and tribulations;

> Anne was returning from her first cosmetology class.
> He'd signed her up that morning, her third in the
> city…[she longed to escape,] her younger brother's
> drowning, her stepbrother's departure from their
> seaside village, perhaps to avoid the waters that had
> taken her brother's life, their respective parents' death
> from either chagrin or hunger or both, her recent
> move to the city to join her older brother… (Danticat
> 209 & 215).

Therefore, it is effortless for Anne to migrate from the island when, "The day after she met her daughter's father, he used most of the money he was keeping in his mattress to procure them passage on a Pan American flight to New York" (240).

Anne represents islanders' consistent migration and aptness to leave behind their struggles on the island.

Similar to Anne's character, Danticat presents Romain. The adolescent, Romain, displays the fact that once an opportunity for migration arises, islanders are willing to uproot from the Caribbean. After failed attempts to encounter his father, Romain realizes that the sole representation of loved ones, without a parental representation, on the island isn't sufficient and turns to one's desire to migrate; "Roamain's mother was away…in Curacao." "It was becoming clear to me that Romain was leaving, going off someplace where I couldn't follow him… 'I'm leaving the country,' 'I'm getting out tonight…' [and since Romain's departure,] his mother never returned…" (Danticat 149, 160-161, 164).

Even the young populates of the Caribbean share the same thoughts and aspirations as the old, rich, and experienced; further expanding the presence of the commonality of migration amongst Caribbean people.

Chapter 1: The Underlying Desperation of Migration

The consistency of migration within the Caribbean is only half of the problem; the desperation inclined with it, is another major issue within the Caribbean. Though Romain's case is one that appears to be more subtle, many Caribbean people find that they reach the point of desperation in order to have some type of eventual connection to the Westernized world; "Ten years ago her parents had sold everything they owned from what passed for a lower-middle-class neighborhood to one on the edge of a slum, in order to send her to nursing school abroad" (Danticat 62-63). Danticat is displaying here several concepts: 1) the consistency of Caribbean migration, 2) desperation, and 3) the class system of Caribbean lifestyle.

In comparison, Barbados native Austin Clarke explores the desperate-desire of migrants within the Caribbean, especially Barbados. Clarke descriptively narrates a young man's determination to migrate to Canada in fulfillment of his educational and athletic goals from the

Caribbean. He is determined to travel away to school despite leaving behind loved ones, and a dying father. "Let him die. I am leaving this island place. And let him die with his claim on my life... 'Don't take long to return back, child! Do not tarry too long. Come back again soon...and don't forget that you were borned right here, pon this rock, pon this island...." (Clarke 224, 227). Like many migrates, he is still persistent to migrate to Canada. Clarke represents that Caribbean natives are so determined to migrate to European countries that they will do so "by any means necessary." "And it is the next day, mid-morning, and I am sitting in the Seawell Airport terminal, waiting to be called to board the plane. I am leaving. My father, is he dead yet?" (Clarke 226). As implied at the end of the piece, the young man unchangingly leaves the island. Clarke is able to capture the essence of the idea, motive, and passion of migration by Caribbean natives, while causally supporting the notion of an inadequate education and livelihood throughout the Caribbean; compared to European colonizing nations.

Furthermore, a migrant's desperation is apparent through his/her sustainability of the traveling process; "JA customs officer has eyes deep in passport, behind desk, trying to figure out whether dis a banana boat passport or what…Why do they want to leave? tourist wonders… Temper crackle in dis small island. Sufferation pon di land. Tribulation upon tribulation" (Silvera 400). Caribbean writers are able to easily narrate a new migrates overwhelming immigrant experience at the airport, so accurately, because this is the true time when he/she encounters their new life, and it symbolizes the leaving behind the "old" Caribbean life for the "new" Europeanized world, and they themselves have experienced it. "They were searching her suitcase…One meager bag…contained the few things she'd been unable to part with…Neighbors who had traveled before had told her to gift-wrap everything so it wouldn't be reopened at the airport in New York. Now the customs man was tearing her careful wrapping to shreds as he barked questions at her in mangled Creole…By the time he was done with her luggage, she had little left" (Danticat 39-40). In consideration of the travel experience of migrates, why do Caribbeans anticipate migration so much? Why has it become part of their existence?

Chapter 2: **The Devastation of the Caribbean's Natural**

Resources

The deprived/poor lifestyle that plagues the Caribbean is one major factor that leads to the consistent and massive amounts of migration. As implied in the works of Caribbean authors, this unfortunate lifestyle is a result of the devastation of the Caribbean's natural resources. Centuries ago, "Gold was one of the commodities traded by Arawaks, but it was prized only as an ornament," and "with gold reserves to be mined, [and] crops to be farmed,…" Now the Caribbean is only a residue of the prosperous land it once was (Hamlyn 27 & 29).

The Caribbean is known for its natural resources of gold, sugar, tobacco, spices, and cotton, to name a few. These natural resources were strongly devastated as a result of the settlement of the Europeans who wanted and attained domination of the Caribbean, since their discoveries in the 15th century. Later, "The West Indian sugar planter held the known world with his gaze and made 'good' with the extensive array of goods produced… 'Factory in the field,' the sugar mill was probably Europe's largest industrial complex in the 16th and 17th centuries…" (Beckles 779). In addition, "By 1763, when the Seven Years War between the British and French came to an end, Britain owned five out of the 10 most profitable sugar islands (Jamaica alone produced over 30,000 tonnes a year) and their planters had become some of the empire's most prosperous and influential men," however "by the late 18th century many [Plantations/lands] had been overused, exhausting the soil," ultimately leading to the life of poverty that many Caribbeans are faced with presently (Hamlyn 35). "When people in England and America say slums, Trinidadians say barrack-yards. Probably the word is a relic of the days when England relied as much on garrisons of soldiers as on her fleet to protect her valuable sugar-producing colonies…[now the land is] hopelessly inadequate water-closet, unmistakable to the nose if not to the eye…No longer do the barrack-yarders live the picturesque life of twenty-five years ago" (James 35). Trinidadian author

C.L.R James recollects this radical economical change within the Caribbean since the departure of the Europeans.

Haitian author Edwidge Danticat, as a literary representative of the Caribbean experience, highlights in <u>The Dew Breaker,</u> the various signs and situations that Caribbeans experience as a representation of their poverty-stricken lives. Nadine, a nurse in the novel, finds that her family back in Haiti depends on the money she sends back home in order to make a decent living; "…your father ['s…] health is, always, unreliable… He and I both thank you for the money you sent last month. We know it is difficult for you, but we are very grateful…She had raided her savings to wire double the usual amount…" (Danticat 53-54). Regardless of one's age or health, economically he/she would still struggle because most of the Caribbean's natural resources were the main profit and employer; " 'C'est a' ce prix qu'ils mangent du sucre en Europe'… 'I'm sharing with you Voltaire's words,'… 'I tell you that in Europe they eat sugar with our blood in it and you mock me with a colonial title'" (Danticat 153). Caribbean people are aware of their history under the Europeans' slavery, which is why it is difficult for them to live underprivileged lives when they are informed of the riches gained through the Caribbean in European nations.

Danticat and Barbados native Paule Marshall in "Ta Da-duh, in Memoriam," further displays the poverty of islanders through their excitement, and dependence on small resources and their aspirations;

> Over the weeks I told her about refrigerators, radios, gas stoves, elevators, trolley cars, wringer washing machines, movies, airplanes, the cyclone at Coney island, subways, toasters, electric lights: 'At night, see, all you have to do is flip this little switch on the wall and all the lights in the house go on. Just like that. Like magic. It's like turning on the sun at night.'... 'tell me [more]' [eagerly said the Caribbean little girl] (Marshall 165).

The president of the republic would drive through my

town on New Year's Eve and throw money from the

window of his big shiny black car...When we heard

that the president was coming, we would clean or

entire house, dust our cedar table, and my father

would stay home from the sea in case the president

chose to get out of the car and walk into our house, to

offer something extra, a bag of rice, a pound of beans,

a gallon of corn oil, a promise of future entrance to

the medical school or the agricultural school in

Damien...(Danticat 170- 171).

The lack of resources that Caribbean people face daily,

starkly contrasts the resources that many people in European

countries have. Some islanders find that these circumstances

result in them magnifying their deprived lives to both

themselves and foreigners, inadvertently, asking for help.

Europeans ruined these islands, exhausted their soil

on single crop agriculture, drove their economies into

dead ends. Caribbeans have fought hard to have

nations, to be free men and women, to erase the

stigma of slavery and take their place in the

community of nations. But it was only when their

Caribbean holdings were no longer profitable that

Europeans relinquished the, just as slavery had ended

only when the plantation economy was no longer

profitable (Kurlansky vii).

The devastation of the Caribbean's natural resources of the

18th century has put Caribbean's in great dependence on other

nations and causes suffrage from a lack of jobs; increasing

Caribbeans common thread of migration.

Chapter 3: Unemployment: A Search for Stability

Unemployment brings down the quality of life of any person, or a nation that is plagued with this misfortune. Throughout the Caribbean, the inhabitants find that they are subject to unemployment, which is a result of the devastated/destroyed plantations, and short-lived minimal factories. "To many Caribbeans, going aboard was not a question of emigrating but simply a matter of survival…[they] remembering their countries that had no place for them, no way for them to earn an income…" (Kurlansky x, 224).

Caribbeans find comfort in each other, in knowing that most of the people are jobless, and aspire to migrate. Caribbeans console each other by saying, "There's tons of people like you [and I] in this city. Half of them need a job" (Danticat 47). It is no secret that life in the Caribbean is difficult, as there are very little means of income for the inhabitants; "He explained why he [Haitian immigrant] had two jobs…he needed to support both himself here, and her in

Port-au-Prince" (Danticat 46). Caribbeans want to be self-sufficient, which is why they all want to migrate for more opportunities. But since this dream isn't a reality for them all, many islanders have resulted in dependence on family aboard, and/or entrepreneurship.

Author Makeda Silvera in "Caribbean Chameleon," captures the struggle to find sufficient employment in the Caribbean through descriptive aspirations and narratives of daily labors; "Praying that in five years, no more kneeling to wash floor, no more scrubbing clothes, replace that with washing machine, vacuum cleaner…Goodbye slave wage, stale food, rancid meat, tear-up clothes, rag man, turn' cornmeal, dry dust" (Silvera 400-401). The speaker aspires to leave the Caribbean soon for a more profitable life.

Similarly, Danticat portrays this struggle of employment in, The Dew Breaker: "It's the maid. She's a young Cuban woman who is overly polite, making up for lack of English with deferential gestures… 'A Haitian-born actress with her own American television show. We have really come far'… 'I've been making [wedding] dresses since Haiti'…" (Danticat 8, 11, & 126). These jobs though only a few represent the self-employment and jobs of peasantry that many islanders are subject to as a result of the lack of adequate employment in the Caribbean. It is theorized that when the European presence in the Caribbean lessened, islanders had very little to no means of employment/ compensation because the European empire was no longer providing funding. Caribbean writers constantly display this everlasting challenge of finding meaningful, self-fulfilling employment, while living in the Caribbean.

Lack of employment is often the justifiable reason for migrating; "'What's going to happen to your club when all the players gone away?' 'All? All the players?' 'Well, the stars. Prince, your fast bowler going to Canada. Murray going. Ali gone to the States'… They going to study. They have to think about their future. They have to get their education. Just now, just from the fellars who leave and go away from Cunaripo and they come back with their BAs and

MAs and Ph dees they could run the government' (Lovelace 231). Here author Earl Lovelace, like most Caribbean writers, presents the reality that islanders must migrate in hopes of a sufficient education and employment. Many of the players on the cricket team, represented by Lovelace, leave behind their athletic passions to seek the economic opportunities that aren't available in the Caribbean. However, looking at the broader situation— economic instability in the Caribbean, in reference to its people and employment and educational opportunities. Social mobility is oftentimes not a reality for the lower class citizens. In addition, a failed Caribbean government is represented in the works of several Caribbean writers, to be the leading cause of the economic instability and intertwined constant migration of Caribbeans.

Chapter 4: The Predetermined failure of the
Caribbean Government

Edwidge Danticat's The Dew Breaker, emphasizes on the dictatorship of Haiti's Papa Doc- Duvalier's regime, as a causing factor to the migration issues continuously plaguing Haiti; "Constant had created his death squad after a military coup had sent Haiti's president into exile. Constant's thousands of disciplines had sought to silence the president's followers by circling entire neighborhoods with gasoline, setting houses on fire, and shooting fleeing residents" (Danticat 79). However, this instability of government and order throughout Haiti and other islands began centuries prior to the violence and destruction of Duvalier's coup.

Former uneducated slaves had to establish and maintain a government and its people, during the demolishment of slavery. The lack of knowledge on the part of the slaves who were banned from learning to read and write, had to figure out for the first time the functions of government, while occupying a destructed and disabled land. Jamaican artist, Bunny Wailer shares his insights on how: Caribbeans were struggling against enormous obstacles to build nations. With seemingly everything against them, they never gave up, never lost faith... 'Yeah, mon, the Caribbean try to make countries. It's a kind of magic. Making something from magic. Making something from nothing'....(Kurlansky vii).

With the end of slavery under the Europeans, in the Caribbean, Caribbeans were left to learn how to govern their nation on their own without the financial support or guidance of the European empire overseas. This ethical issue will continue to be their downfall in establishing a strong -structured government. However, the underlying issues are the ideologies that were implanted in the minds of the inhabitants by the Europeans, ultimately displaying their rooted "mind control:"

The ideology of racism which at that time was not clearly articulated, but which rooted itself in the Caribbean;

34

the social ideology of patriarchy which assumed the superior political and intellectual capacity of men over women; an intolerant Christian ideology which defined other religions as primitive subtypes; an expansionist imperialist consciousness that focused on total materialism as the way forward for mankind…People of European ancestry continue to dominate resource ownership in Caribbean societies despite their loss of political leadership…they did…imposition of international blockade, refusal to grant financial assistance, and general economic sabotage. No modern nation can now survive without international connections (Beckles 786).

Caribbeans, as the recipients of the failed Caribbean parliament, are aware of all its malfunctions, promoting their inevitable migration;

> "We have fallen asleep under a dictatorship headed by a pudgy thirty- four-year old man and his glamorous wife…Now the population was going after those militiamen, those macoutes, with the determination of an army in the middle of its biggest battle to date….

A great many of our fathers had also died in the

dictatorship's prisons, and others had abandoned us

altogether to serve the regime… [They] had beaten

them up and stolen money and property from most of

them and had put many of their relatives in jail or in

the grave…" (Danticat 140-142).

The Haitian government represents the corruption,

dishonesty, and disorder that takes place throughout the

Caribbean's political system. Many of the leaders, as

described as uneducated on governing a nation functionally,

therefore making it harder for the inhabitants to live there.

The dictator, Duvalier, created lots of destruction on the

island. Years after the independence of the various Caribbean

islands from European rule, Caribbeans still suffer from its

effects economically, and morally. Caribbeans are in a

consistent struggle and search for a productive government,

as they are fed up. "Graffiti was going up everywhere. Down

with the departed president and his wife! Down with poverty!

Down with suffering! Down with everything you can imagine" (Danticat 149).

Overall, it is clear that the Caribbean government was set up for failure by and at the departure of the Europeans, who still hold a grudge against the revolutionaries. It appears as though the Caribbean government will never fully succeed. This issue of a failing government serves as one of the main subjects of Caribbean literature because the authors' writings are reflections of their respective societies.

Author "George Lamming, however, has consistently made the wider point with respect to the empty formality of constitutionally independent nation-states, that those who govern don't rule" (Beckles 787). Migration to nations that are ruled by European forces are more stable politically and incorporate the economic wealth that was gained during the European exploration and slave trade, therefore being the only other option for Caribbean people.

Chapter 5: Caribbean People, an Everlasting Displaced Race?

Lastly, this common thread of migration throughout the Caribbean is resulted from the overall displacement characteristic that Caribbean people had to intake in the past. When considering the idea of consistent migrating from the Caribbean, one should analyze the demographics of the region and its effect on those inhabitants.

The Caribbean occupies the Caribbean Sea, and is made-up of various demographics, cultures, and island- based histories. The Caribbean is said to have a majority of African ancestry: "In the French Caribbean, Anglophone Caribbean and Dutch Caribbean, there are minorities of mixed-race and European people of French, English, Dutch and Portuguese ancestry," as well as those of Chinese and Indian ancestry that arrived in the 19th century (Hamlyn). In addition, it is common to encounter the Mulattos, Syrians, Lebanese, and European races in the Caribbean, as migration and mixture of races has increased in previous years. These varieties of people display the years of interaction and changes that have taken place in the Caribbean. From the early years of the Arawak and Carib Indians, to the settlement of the Europeans, then the transportation of African slaves, and the many other integrating races, makes the Caribbean a collage of various religions, heritage, teachings, languages, foods, and many more; Ultimately resulting in Caribbean people internalizing notion that they are not true inhabitants of the Caribbean, and have very little tolerance for the sufferings that they endure, rationalizing their want to uproot. Author Naipaul explains the relevancy of this factor when he explains that, "Almost every major civilization in the world was brought to the Caribbean in order to sustain the conditions for the colonial economic growth...There were white people, not all of them English; and the Portuguese and the Chinese, at one time also immigrants like us [Indians from India]...were the people we called Spanish, '*pagnols*, mixed people of warm brown complexions who came from the Spanish time (Naipaul 483). But, what is the exact relationship between the diverse make-up of the Caribbean and their migration? The West Indian is a "futuristic individual, linked to all major civilizations. They are the first products of the modern world system" (Beckles 786).

Furthermore, white people represented power and money because they controlled the lands, and the operations of the early centuries. Therefore, Caribbeans have internalized the ideology of dependence on the white man's wealth, which has led to the large numbers of Caribbean immigrants to European lands because they (Caribbean people) were only settlers of the island, never fully freed or given the necessary provisions by the exiting Europeans, to establish and maintain a sufficient living on the islands.

Chapter 6: Conclusion

There are innumerable reasons why peoples of the world immigrate to other nations. It is often believed that the world wasn't created to have borders but a space to thrive and multiply, while living in the greatness of the earth.

This text, simply touches on some of the reasons for the constant migration of peoples of the Caribbean, but in no way is represented as a totality. From sufferings of poverty, a devastated economy, failed government, corruption, lack of educational and employment opportunities, Caribbeans have been suffering for centuries and turn the former colonizing nations. Are they at fault? No. Caribbean writers, as displayed in this text are of the same people, cultures and ideologies that they portray in their pieces. Therefore, accurately relaying the causes for their and other Caribbeans' migration. The Caribbean, as well as other places in the world, can be viewed as a "melting pot," so it is understandable that over time, Caribbean people want to explore the world and travel away from the trials and tribulations which their homelands are subject to. However, the most meaningful factor of migration, that is often overlooked, is where their true loyalty lies.

Caribbeans, as displaced people that are "fed-up" with the conditions of their homelands, turn to European lands for stability only to support their families and lives back in the Caribbean, as the same is for the authors whose main subject is of the Caribbean. The Caribbean will always be home for Caribbean people, but the odds against them are high. Caribbean people seek the same comfort that many Americans, Europeans, etc., are given the opportunity to live; therefore as humans they aspire and long for their opportunity to live a self-sufficient, meaningful life.

Luggage Store (Haiti)

Street Vendor

Local community store

Street Vender

Traditional Haitian Meal: Steamed fish, vegetables, rice, and black bean sauce

Traditional Haitian Meal: Spaghetti, hot dogs in sauce

Clothes Street Vender

Hotel

Hair Salon in Haiti (Outside)

Hair Salon in Haiti (Inside)

Traffic in Haiti (Midday)

Home in a local village in Haiti

Home in a local village in Haiti

Homes Community in Haiti

Homes Community in Haiti

Street Vender

Local Bridge in Haiti

Church afar in Haiti

University entrance in Haiti

Playing Soccer in an open Field (Haiti)

… And just like that, the voyage begins.

Works Cited

Beckles, McD. Hilary. "Capitalism, Slavery and Caribbean

    Modernity." Callaloo 20.4

    (Autumn 1997): 777-789. <u>JSTOR</u> Mercy Libs., NY

    December 2009.

Brown, Stewart, and John Wickham, Eds. <u>The Oxford Book</u>

    <u>of Caribbean Short Stories</u>.

    Oxford: Oxford University Press, 1999

Clarke, Austin. "Leaving this Island Place." <u>The Oxford</u>

    <u>Book of Caribbean Short Stories</u>. Ed. Stewart Brown

    and John Wickham. Oxford: Oxford University Press,

    1999. 220-227.

Chancy, Myriam J.A. "The Challenge to Center: Caribbean

    Literature." American Literary History 13.2 (Summer

    2001): 329-342. <u>JSTOR</u> Mercy Libs., NY 1

    December 2009.

Danticat, Edwidge. <u>The Dew Breaker</u>. New York: Knopf,

    2004. 242 pages.

De Las Casas, Bartolome. <u>A Short Account of the</u>

<u>Destruction of the Indies</u>. London,

England: Penguin Books, 1992.

"Fact Sheet: Biden-Harris Administration Announces New

Border Enforcement Actions."

The White House, The United States Government, 5

Jan. 2023,

<u>https://www.whitehouse.gov/briefing-room/statement</u>

<u>s-releases/2023/01/05/fact-sheet-biden-harris-adminis</u>

<u>tration-announces-new-border-enforcement-actions/</u>.

Hamlyn, James. <u>Fodor's Exploring Caribbean.</u> New York:

Fodor's Travel Publications,

2002.

James, C.L.R. "Triumph." <u>The Oxford Book of Caribbean</u>

<u>Short Stories</u>. Ed. Stewart

Brown and John Wickham. Oxford: Oxford

University Press, 1999. 35-50.

Kurlansky, Mark. <u>A Continent of Islands: Searching for the</u>

Caribbean Destiny. Canada:Berkeley Book, 1992.

Lovelace, Earl. "Victory and the Blight." The Oxford Book

of Caribbean Short Stories.

Ed. Stewart Brown and John Wickham. Oxford:

Oxford University Press, 1999.

228-235.

Marshall, Paule. "To Da-duh, in Memoriam." The Oxford

Book of Caribbean Short

Stories. Ed. Stewart Brown and John Wickham.

Oxford: Oxford University

Press, 1999. 159-169.

Martinez, Kathia. "US, Panama and Colombia Aim to Stop

Darien Gap Migration." MSN, 10 Apr. 2023,

https://www.msn.com/en-us/news/world/us-panama-a

nd-colombia-aim-to-stop-darien-gap-migration/ar-AA

19K7iB?ocid=msedgdhp&pc=U531&cvid=dbd2c399

6f6c4112b07212f7e70ebc55&ei=7.

Naipaul, V.S. "Two Worlds." Modern Language Association

117.3 (May 2002): 479-486. <u>JSTOR</u> Mercy Libs., NY

4 March 2009.

Silvera, Makeda. "Caribbean Chameleon." <u>The Oxford Book</u>

<u>of Caribbean Short</u> <u>Stories</u>. Ed. Stewart Brown and

John Wickham. Oxford: Oxford University

Press, 1999. 399-402.

Text Description

This text is a literary essay that evaluates the causes of Caribbean migration, consistently, over the decades. The background reads that the issue of Caribbean migration is evolving, as migration is increasing with time. Many theorists have tried to determine the factors that are contributing to the increasing numbers of Caribbean immigrants to the "States" and other European nations; governed by the same government they've driven out and attained independence from in the past. Despite the Caribbean's attainment of national independence from Europeans, it appears through written and oral discourse, that the Caribbean islands and its people haven't fully acquired independence from the inferior conditions of their past; from which they are still suffering economically and socially. This short analysis, with photos included, will analyze the literature of Caribbean- migrant- authors, while exploring their theories underlying the inferior economic conditions, lifestyle differences, and the consistent migration of the

Caribbean Islands.